REAL ESTATE LAW IN SPAIN

Purchase, possession, rent and taxes.
The guide from your Spanish Lawyers.

MARÍA SANTOS ACEDO

Spanish Lawyer

CHRISTOPH SANDER

Spanish Lawyer and Tax Advisor

January 2021
Copyright © 2021 Sander, Santos & Partners S.L.P.
www.s-s.partners

ISBN- 9798649308687

INTRODUCTION

When buying property abroad, it is particularly important to have basic information about laws and taxes in advance.

This book informs you understandable about the most important legal and tax aspects of property in Spain, so the individual chapters deal not only with the purchase of properties, also with your property, rental income, tourist rental etc. Regarding the purchase of real estate, this book not only gives you important legal information, but also describes the whole process from a practical point of view using a checklist to buy real estate, which you can use after reading the book for your own purchase.

Finally, you will also find information on the reasons for residence in Spain and the administrative and fiscal consequences of the property on your tax residence.

About the author:

María Santos Acedo is a registered lawyer who completed her law studies at the University of Seville. She has been living and working abroad for 2 years after studying law, specifically in Ireland and after that, she completed her master's degree at the University of Malaga.

INDEX

FOREWORD: DATA AND FACTS

Even if the objective of this book is to respond to the legal, administrative and fiscal aspects related to the purchase and possession of real estate in Spain, this text is intended to provide you with some basic facts and information before choosing your new property.

For emigrants and lovers of Spain, the temperate climate, the calm life, and the good people in Spain are decisive. However, there are several tax and administrative obligations in case of a longer stay or even the reason for residence.

After the chapters on buying, owning, and renting real estate, the last chapter of this book contains basic information about your choice of residence and the associated consequences.

Before that, a few words about the climate, the people, and the country of Spain.

Spain is divided into 17 Autonomous Communities and two autonomous cities located on the African continent (Ceuta and Melilla). Especially for migrants, it should be noted that several Autonomous Communities have second official languages, particularly in the north and east. Even you can do an administrative procedure in Spanish, also in areas with their own official languages like in Catalonia and the Balearic Islands, the knowledge of this local languages is often important.

Weather is another important point when choosing a new home to reside. Spain has a diversity of climates depending on where we are:

- Atlantic climate with frequent rainfall and a moderate climate, both in winter and summer, on the North Atlantic coast: Galicia, Asturias, Cantabria, Pais Vasco and Navarra.

- Oceanic-continental climate in central Spain, with cold winters, regular snowfall and hot summers: Castilla y León, Madrid, La Rioja, Navarra, Castilla-La Mancha.

- Continental Mediterranean climate with rainfall, especially in spring and autumn in Catalonia, Valencia and Murcia.

- Mediterranean climate with mild winter and high temperatures in summer, in Catalonia, the Balearic

Island, Valencia and Andalusia.

- Subtropical climate in the Canary Island, with mild temperatures almost all year round.

Spain is an extremely popular country for immigrants from Europe, South America and Asia due to its climate, language, customs and gastronomy.

In 2019, 5.036.878 foreigners lived permanently in Spain, which is approximately 10.7% of the total population of Spain. Especially on the coast, the proportion of foreigners is often much higher and reaches up to 40% of the population in some municipalities, especially on the islands and in some parts of Andalusia and Valencia. Due to the severe economic crisis and high unemployment in the years 2009 to 2016, the number of Central Europeans living in Spain fell sharply.[1]

1. Morocco	714.239	
2. Romania	671.233	
3. England	287.292	
4. Italy	244.148	
5. Ecuador	199.540	
6. China	190.624	
7. Germany	138.642	

---

[1] Instituto Nacional de Estadísticas.

I. START IN SPAIN

1. The Spanish NIE number

Spaniards, like all other Europeans, can buy, own and rent real estate in Spain without any restrictions. The only requirement is administrative nature and consists of requesting the Spanish foreigner identification number (NIE). As soon as you have the NIE, nothing stands in the way of buying a home, when carrying out any administrative act before the State Tax Administration Agency, or before any other authority.

The NIE is often wrongly equated with the term "residence". It is just a personal identification number. If you meet the requirements to apply for residence or to establish your permanent residence in Spain, at the time you apply for your residence you can request the NIE.

To apply for residency + NIE, several conditions must be met since 2012. For more information on how to apply for residency, see the next section.

In the case of not fulfilling the necessary requirements to request your "residence" but you need a NIE to carry out administrative acts in Spain (for example, purchase of property) without wanting to establish your residence place in Spain, you can submit your request to the National Police, the Tax Administration and the Spanish diplomatic missions in your country at any time.

If you are a foreigner, the NIE is necessary in Spain in any case if you want to buy a property, to file tax returns, etc. to carry out administrative acts in which you need to identify yourself.

Required documents:

- ✓ Model (EX-15) completed and signed.
- ✓ DNI or passport (original and copy).
- ✓ Indication and, if necessary, proof of the reason for the request: personal, commercial, family.
- ✓ Proof of payment of the fee of approximately €10.

Practical information for the application:

✓ Make an appointment online and take the printed appointment confirmation with you to the authority. Select in the menu: "POLICIA-CERTIFICADOS Y ASIGNACIÓN NIE".

You can find the link for online appointment reservation at the bottom of the page.[2]

✓ Fill out the payment slip online and present it to any Spanish bank for payment before your appointment. With the mechanical stamp of the ATM or the stamp of the bank, the payment slip can be submitted directly to your appointment and it is not necessary to visit the authority again. In the catalog of services, choose: "Asignación de Número de Identidad de Extranjero (NIE) a instancia del interesado.":

Autorización excepcional de entrada o estancia.

Asignación de Número de Identidad de Extranjero (NIE) a instancia del interesado.

Certificados o informes emitidos a instancia del interesado.

You can find the payment slip under the link at the bottom of the page.[3]

---

[2] https://sede.administracionespublicas.gob.es/icpplus
[3] https://sede.policia.gob.es:38089/Tasa790_012/ImpresoRellenar

✓ Download the application form EX-15[4] before your appointment and fill it out and sign it in duplicate with you to your appointment. You will find the link to the form at the end of the page.

Delimitation of terms:

Especially for people residing abroad and who do not intend to establish their fiscal domicile in Spain, it is important to request only the NIE number, but not to register in the Central Registry of Foreigners as "resident". If you plan to establish your residence in Spain, applying for this "residence" is one of the first and most important steps.

---

[4] https://sede.policia.gob.es/portalCiudadano/extranjeria/pr_cer_residen.html

2. Application for the Spanish "residence"

Since 2012, the reception of the Spanish "residence" is only possible if various conditions are met: pensioners, students, holders of employment contracts, independent workers, relatives of residents, etc. It is often confused with receiving the Spanish NIE number.

The inscription in the Central Registry of Foreigners can be requested personally at any time to the National Police of your place of residence. After the payment of the €10,60 fee, and the submission of the application form and documentation, the registration certificate will be issued if the requirements are met. Please note that this certificate is not the "green card" as the latter is only issued to non-European foreigners.

To register with the National Police Station as a "resident" and, therefore, live in Spain for more than 3 months, one of the following requirements must be met:

1. Have an employment contract:

If you have a valid employment contract, you can register as a "resident" without further ado. It is enough to present your employment contract, working life or registration certificate in Social Security.

This point also includes posted workers, cross-border workers, pensioners or officials and their dependents insured through the health insurance of the country of each foreigner who wishes to move to Spain. It will be enough to send the European model S1.

2. Be registered as self-employed:

If you are registered as a self-employed worker in Spain, you can also obtain "residence" by submitting your registration in the Spanish Social Security system and registering on the list of economic activities (Census of Economic Activities). It is important to obtain the NIE to register with the Tax Administration and Social Security and you must request it in advance. The possibility of receiving "residence" is interesting because the Spanish Social Security contribution rate for the new self-employed is considerably reduced.

Therefore, it is very possible that the first year you only pay 60 euros monthly contribution, which covers both your family's full health insurance and the payment to the pension fund.

3. If you are a student:

If you study in Spain, you can also register as a "resident" if you have enough coverage in relation to health insurance, study at an educational institution financed or recognized by the Spanish Ministry of Education, and prove that you have sufficient financial resources.

4. Relatives of "residents":

Members of the "resident" family can also generally register as residents if they prove the family relationship and economic dependency. Regarding health insurance coverage, they are fundamentally insured in Spain through the "resident" as "beneficiary". If a family member contributes to the Spanish Social Security system through independent or dependent work in Spain, the whole family is financed with health insurance.

5. Have enough financial resources:

If your case is not mentioned in any of the preceding paragraphs, you can still obtain "residence" if you can prove that you have health insurance (private or state) and sufficient financial resources for both you and your family. These economic resources can be proven through different means such as income from rentals and leases, saving accounts, credit cards, etc.

As soon as you obtain your "residence", you will become a resident citizen in our country, which entails a series of administrative and fiscal obligations (tax returns, model 720, etc.). It should be noted that, even without "residence", in some cases you already consider yourself a resident in Spain and, therefore, must tax your worldwide income before the competent administration.

Required documents:

- ✓ Form (EX-18) completed and signed by duplicate.
- ✓ Registration certificate from the City Council (Volante).
- ✓ Possibly. Your NIE certificate or NIE card.
- ✓ Identity card or passport (original and copy).
- ✓ Proof of payment of the fee of approx. €10.
- ✓ Proof of fulfillment of one of the mentioned requirements (employee or self-employed, pensioner or financial means and health insurance).

Practical information for applying for the residence:

- ✓ Make an appointment online and take the printed appointment confirmation with you to the authority. Select in the menu: "POLICIA-CERTIFICADO UE". You can find the link for online appointment reservation at the bottom of the page[5].
- ✓ Complete the payment slip online and present it to any Spanish bank for payment before your appointment. With the mechanical stamp of the ATM or the stamp of the bank, the payment slip can be submitted directly to

---

[5] https://sede.administracionespublicas.gob.es/icpplus

your appointment and it is not necessary to visit the authority again.

In the catalog of services, select: "Certificado de registro de residente comunitario o Tarjeta de residencia de familiar de un ciudadano de la Unión":

.TIE que documenta la autorización de residencia de larga duración o de residencia de larga duración-UE.

.Certificado de registro de residente comunitario o Tarjeta de residencia de familiar de un ciudadano de la Unión.

You can find the payment slip under the link at the bottom of the page.[6]

Download the application form EX-18[7] before your appointment and fill it out and sign it in duplicate with you to your appointment. You will find the link to the form at the end of the page.

---

[6] https://sede.policia.gob.es:38089/Tasa790_012/ImpresoRellenar

[7] https://sede.policia.gob.es/portalCiudadano/extranjeria/EX18.pdf

3. Differences: Residence and NIE

As mentioned in the previous sections, sooner or later all people living in Spain come across the term's residence, place of residence and NIE. The correct differentiation of the various terms is particularly important to be able to carry out the various administrative acts without incurring any type of non-compliance.

NIE:

The foreigner's identification number is also the personal identification number in Spain and is required for almost all administrative acts. Possession of the NIE is often used incorrectly as a presumption of residence, producing no effect in this regard. In several cases, it is even necessary to request the NIE if you are not yet in Spain (for example, for the purchase of properties, payment of taxes, etc.).

Residence:

Basically, the place of residence has to be equated with the term "residence", but it often refers incorrectly to registration in the Central Register of Foreign Nationals in the Police Station.

If you reside in Spain, you are considered a resident for administrative and tax purposes, even if you are not registered as a "resident" in the Central Register of Foreign Nationals. It should be noted that the administrative residence, with some exceptions, is the tax residence. You will be considered a resident if you are in Spain for more than 183 days a year. In terms of administration, it is generally considered for this purpose if it is registered in the Resident Registry Office (population register) and in the Central Registry of Foreign as "resident".

Unlike the Population Census, the Central Register of Foreign can only be entered if several requirements are met.

For example, if you have a permanent stay in both Spain and Germany and you are in Spain for half a year, you are free to choose your residence place, because depending on the country in which you stay for half a year and one day (183 days), is a resident there.

Regardless of the administrative domicile, the fiscal domicile has much broader consequences. As soon as you are a tax resident, you must tax your worldwide income in Spain and comply with the corresponding tax obligations (for example, tax returns, model 720).

It should be noted that the Spanish tax office invests considerable resources to determine who is considered a resident in Spain and who is only in Spain temporarily or on vacation. It is very possible that the Tax Agency checks if your children go to school in Spain, if you make regular money movements in Spain (cash withdrawals, card payments on purchases), if you regularly pay electricity, water or phone etc.

4. The electronic signature

Thanks to the electronic signature, many administrative tasks can be performed from your home via on-line. Spain is one of the most advanced European Union of the Member States in the field of electronic administration. Unlike other European countries, the electronic signature is available free of charge to all Spaniards and residents in Spain and offers quick and easy access to the administrative portals of the various authorities. Various steps can be taken, such as paying taxes, checking the points of the driving license, finding out about the status of contributions to the Spanish Social Security system. Another advantage is that many certificates can be printed at home immediately after the request, so it is no longer necessary to request it in person at the offices of the competent authority. To obtain the electronic signature, you only need the Spanish NIE number, which you will receive request it and comply with the requirements set out on the page.

Electronic signature request: The electronic signature request is made on-line on the website of the "National Currency and Stamps Manufactured" (FNMT). To make the request, you just need to know 3 simple steps; it is important that the request is made from the same device from which you want to download the electronic signature. Once you get your NIE number, follow these steps to request the signature:

1. Enter your NIE on the FNMT website and note the confirmation number.[8]

2. Go to one of the official government agencies or delegations to confirm your identity. You will need your NIE, your identity card or passport and the confirmation number you received from FNMT by email. The easiest way to verify your identity is to contact the nearest Spanish tax office. In the appointment process, you will enter your zip code to find out where the nearest delegation of the tax office is located.[9]

3. Two hours after your identity has been confirmed, you can download your digital signature from the FNMT website by entering your NIE and your confirmation number. Most browsers install the signature directly when downloading.[10]

---

[8] https://www.sede.fnmt.gob.es/certificados/persona-fisica
[9] https://www.sede.fnmt.gob.es/certificados/persona-fisica
[10] www.sede.fnmt.gob.es/certificados

Examples of using of the electronic signature:

Agencia Tributaria

Tax office:
- Presentation of tax returns.[11]
- Application for residence certificates.[12]
- Economic activities.[13]

GOBIERNO DE ESPAÑA   MINISTERIO DE JUSTICIA

Ministry of Justice:
- Authorization of the powers of the process.[14]
- Request for a criminal record extract.[15]

INSTITUTO NACIONAL DE LA SEGURIDAD SOCIAL

Social Security:
- Pension calculator.[16]
- Read social security contributions.[17]
- Certificaty of working life.[18]

---

[11] www.agenciatributaria.es
[12] www.agenciatributaria.es/Certificados_tributarios.shtml
[13] www.agenciatributaria.gob.es/AEAT.sede/tramitacion/G322.shtml
[14] https://sedejudicial.justicia.es/sje/publico/sjepublico/tramites_y_servicio
[15] www.mjusticia.gob.es/cs/certificado-antecedentes
[16] https://w6.seg-social.es/autocalculo/inicio.do
[17] http://www.seg-social.es/Cotizacionyrecaudac48433/index.htm
[18] http://www.seg-social.es/Internet_1/index.htm?C1=3

Traffic direction:
- License points.[19]
- Ticket payments.[20]

Cadastral office:
-Katasterauszuges Ihrer Immobilie.[21]
- Registration of real estate.[22]

Land Registry
- Request for cadastre.[23]
- Receipt of commercial record extracts.[24]

---

[19] https://sede.dgt.gob.es/es/tramites-y-multas/permiso-por-puntos
[20] https://sede.dgt.gob.es/es/tramites-y-multas/alguna-multa/pago-de-multas/
[21] http://www.sedecatastro.gob.es/
[22] https://www1.sedecatastro.gob.es/ValidacionesGraficas
[23] https://www.registradores.org/registroonline/home.seam
[24] https://www.registradores.org/rmercantil/

II. PURCHASE OF PROPERTY IN SPAIN

1. The Spanish property markets

Today, many foreign citizens want to acquire a property in Spain or have already acquired it. Many of these citizens buy real estate with the intention of moving to live in it, and others as a form of investment through leases. As described in the next chapters, these transactions have far-reaching tax consequences, and the time of purchase plays an important role in most cases.

The Spanish real estate market:

Especially for foreigners, or for people who do not live in Spain, the search for a home through real estate portals can be very striking, seeming a faster and more agile solution to make your dream come true. Although a priori it is a supposedly simpler solution, it should be borne in mind that, in reality, it is the most expensive way to buy a property abroad, because in most cases, real estate agents based in their own country only work with Spanish residents. In some cases, commission and handling costs can triple.

Currently, the most used solution to find the dream property is the online search or the use of web pages that specialize in buying properties. In most cases, these pages act as a viewing portal and therefore do not interfere with the purchase process.

In this case, the ad may has been placed by a real estate agent or directly by the seller.

On-line portals:

In many cases, it is irrelevant whether the search for real estate takes place on national internet portals, as many local real estate agents are now advertising on foreign portals as well.

International portals such as "Immobilienscout24", "kyero.com", "www.immowelt.de", "aplaceinthesun.com" and Spanish portals such as "idealista.com" or "flats.com" can serve as examples. If you speak or understand the Spanish language, it is advisable to extend your search to Spanish portals.

Real estate agent:

If you have already selected a property, the next step is to contact the property agent, as most real estate agent ads are placed on foreign language portals and not directly by the seller.

The advantage here is that the broker knows the market, and even if the seller pays the commission, he is interested in selling the property as quickly as possible and therefore giving price discounts.

Unlike buying from individuals, brokers not only carry out an intermediation activity, but in many cases, they are interested in having a "reservation contract" signed as quickly as possible and making a down payment.

These contracts, generally one or two pages long, are often issued as a "reservation", despite the fact that it is actually a so-called preliminary contract, which in Spain means that you are already committing at a certain time already buy on the terms set forth in this agreement. Not only you can lose the deposit, but you may also be legally obligated to fulfill the contract by paying the full purchase price.

Due to the legal differences that may exist from one country to another in the purchase and sale of housing, the advice of a lawyer who knows the matter is recommended, in order to provide a safe legal service, even if the figure of a real estate agent already exists.

Legal advice:

In any case, before signing any document, it is advisable to contact a Spanish lawyer. In Spain, the lawyer not only helps with the creation and processing of the notarized public deed, but also verifies the preliminary contracts, the legal status of the property in advance (Due Diligence), contact the seller or the broker to obtain the necessary documents for the check, receive data from the Land Registry and the Cadastre office and, in many cases, also help you with the processing and payment of the corresponding taxes.

Due Diligence is performed prior to purchase, using a "due care" risk assessment, see the corresponding chapter.

Choose the correct property:

It is important to consider many factors when buying a home. The price, the size of the property, the location, whether it is an individual home or part of an owner's community, installations and common areas have to be studied. If the seller is up to date with the receipts of Property Tax (IBI), owner's community, electricity, water, gas or garbage. If the home is also used as a second home etc.

2. Real estate purchase process

The sale of real estate in Spain can be done in a private document, through a private sale contract, or in a public document, through a public deed of sale in the notary.

So that there are no unwanted surprises when buying, it is advisable to observe the following points.

Purchase price and payment:

Both the purchase price and the chosen payment method have to be specified in the purchase contract. It should be noted that payments of more than €1,000 in Spain cannot be made in cash if one of the contracting parties is an entrepreneur. Even individuals must refrain from making cash payments and under no circumstances you should make pay without the corresponding receipt.

In practice, an advance of money is usual. The wording of the relevant clauses is crucial here; It has been considered that the initial payment is shown in the contract as a "penitential deposit", because only in this way is a true right of withdrawal constituted.

If the down payment is simply referred to as a "down payment," the buyer may have to honor the contract later despite the loss of the down payment.

Mortgages and other loads:

To ensure that the property is not encumbered by mortgages or other real rights, you can request a simple informative note from the Land Registry. In the section "loads" all those rights that tax the property is listed.

If the house is located within an Owner's Community, it is recommended to request from the Administration a certificate of being up to date with payment on the community receipts. If the owner who wants to sell the home has a debt with the community, the new owner may have to pay the debt after the purchase.

Notarial purchase and registration in the Land Registry:

Unlike other countries, in Spain it is not necessary to register a property to acquire it by purchase, but it is recommended that it be done. To register the purchase in the Land Registry, the sale has to be made in a public deed in a notary, and it is not possible to go directly to the Land Registry with a private sale contract. If said private contract was initially signed, both parties can use the other to be notarized.

It should be noted that the notary only certifies the purchase. To prepare or negotiate the purchase contract, it is always advisable to consult a lawyer specialized in the purchase of properties. As soon as the notarial purchase contract has been concluded, it is recommended to register your rights in the Land Registry without delay. Once this happens, you can assert your property against any third party and thus avoid being victims of possible fraudulent crimes such as double sale or acquisition by unauthorized people. Depending on the Autonomous Community, you have between 20 and 60 days to calculate and pay taxes and, if applicable, in the city government.

There are other incidental purchase costs:

Taxes and Notary and Land Registration fees are often attributed to the home buyer. If you buy from an individual, it is possible to agree who pay costs. If the seller is a real estate company, some expenses cannot be transferred to the buyer, or only to a limited extent.

•

On the other hand, there are also purchases of special properties:

Real estate off-plan or under construction:

Especially in the off-plan home sales area, it should be borne in mind that the property developer must provide you with a compulsory bank guarantee or insurance, of the amounts delivered to a special account designated for this purpose, to ensure the amounts of the possible insolvency from the developer or in the event that the house is not built. These aspects will be treated later. See the corresponding chapter.

Shift utilization property:

If you buy part of a property to use for a certain period per year, there are important special features to consider.

<u>Tourist apartments or hotel rooms:</u>

There are significant usage and rental restrictions.

Real estate purchase process:

In summary, the process of buying a property can be divided into the following steps:

1. Inspection of real estate (Due Diligence).

2. Reservation or pre-contract.

3. The notarial deed of purchase.

4. Payment of taxes.

5. Land Registry.

3. The Due Diligence

With Due Diligence, a risk assessment is carried out with "due attention": The legal situation of the property and the possible risks are analyzed. This preliminary analysis plays an important role both in determining the value of the property and in the legal protection of the buyer.

Most of the Spanish lawyers are not only at your side during the purchase process with sellers, notaries, registries, etc., they also take charge of the prior legal inspection of the property. It must be taken into account if the order form includes the receipt of current extracts from the Land Registry, current graphic descriptions of the Cadastre office, etc., or if you must pay such expenses apart from the fees for the services of the lawyer in question.

Although in any case it is recommended that a specialist carry out this verification, you will find a checklist for the purchase of properties or the Due Diligence below, which contains the most important documents that must be verified before buying.

Simple note from the Land Registry:

In the Land Registry all real estate located in Spain can be registered, as well as the charges and rights that fall on them. This note provides all the necessary information about land (1), the property number (2), the description of the property (3) and the owner (4).

INFORMACIÓN REGISTRAL

1 REGISTRO DE LA PROPIEDAD DE ███████████████

2 FINCA DE ALCALA LA REAL N°: 969
Idufir:(23001000006345)

3 DATOS DE LA FINCA

CASA, marcada con el número cuarenta y uno, de la calle ████████████████ de esta ciudad. El solar es de forma irregular, con una longitud de fachada de seis metros y sesenta centimetros y una profundidad de veintiocho metros y cincuenta centimetros, lo que hace una superficie de ciento treinta y cuatro metros cuadrados. La superficie de solar ocupada por las construcciones es de noventa y un metros

4 TITULARIDAD

TITULAR/CONYUGE	N.I.E.	TOMO LIBRO FOLIO ALTA
███████ JOHANNES	X3819███	1071 523 163 10
KARSTEN████████	X381███	

100,000000% del pleno dominio regimen legal de comunidad.

✓ Property description:

So that you can be sure of what property you are buying, it is important to compare both the property number and the description of the property with what is established in the purchase contract or offer. If the description does not match the 'real one, you can check if it can be updated without problems or if the unregistered buildings can be illegal constructions that cannot be legalized later.

✓ Property owner:

Although there is basically no obligation to register real estate in the Land Registry in Spain, the lack of registration or the purchase of people who are not listed as owners (for example, heirs of the registered owner) can cause costly problems.

✓ Registry loads:

The buyer is only responsible for mortgages, usufruct, etc., if these were registered in the Land Registry before the purchase.

The cadastral extract:

In addition to the Land Registry, which provides binding information on property and rights, there is another registry called Cadastre. While this record it is only for administrative purposes, an examination is necessary as these data provide information on the exact size of the property (5), use, year of construction (3), location (2) and the cadastral value.

The property can be located using the Cadastral Reference number (1), as well as the postal address:

✓ Property description:

The description of the property in the Cadastre office is a summary of the property data relevant to administration. Both the information on the urbanized and underdeveloped area, as well as the registered use (apartment, storage space, commercial premises, agricultural use, etc.) can be compared with that of the Land Registry and with the reality.

✓ Cadastral value:

The cadastral value only appears on the statements requested by the owner, which can also be found in the annual Property Tax (IBI) payment documents. This value depends not only on the aforementioned annual property tax, but also on the tax that will be paid after the purchase.

✓ Protected housing (VPO):

The cadastral statement also shows whether the property is a protected dwelling (VPO). For these properties there are important restrictions in terms of habitability, as well as a fundamental right of first rejection by the corresponding public administration.

Owner's community:

If the cadastral statement shows that we are in front of a house that is part of an owner's community, it has to also be verified if all the pending bills have been paid with the community at the time of the contract. To exclude existing liabilities after purchase, it is advisable to has a certificate issued by the president or administrator of the community, showing that the seller is debt free.

Town Hall:

If there are doubts about the legality of the building, it is advisable to request a corresponding certificate from the City Council on the legality of the building (urban record).

This certificate shows all the structural conditions known to the city government. Therefore, it can be seen if the building permits have been applied for and approved. Whether others may have been requested but rejected or if there are ongoing proceedings against the property or its owner.

Autonomous Community:

Regarding the Autonomous Community in which the property is located, the necessary licenses have to be observed. For example, in the case of renting to tourists (generally for periods less than 2 months), depending on the Autonomous Community, it would be necessary to fulfill several requirements and request the corresponding license. For more information on vacation rentals, see the corresponding chapter.

In addition, in some cases it is advisable to verify the legality of the building at the Autonomous Community level in addition to the certificate of the City Council.

The General Urban Development Plan (PGOU) can be downloaded from the Communities' web pages.

4. Reservation or arras contract

As already mentioned, this type of contract can be found when the purchase is made through a real estate agent. It is a complete and legally binding contract, so legal review and advice is recommended.

When buying through a real estate agent, in many cases these contracts are presented directly by the agent. A legal review is even more important here, since agents do not act independently or disinterested, they have not detailed legal knowledge.

A "reservation contract" prepared and submitted by the real estate agent can quickly become a trap, especially regarding the down payment. Even if the notarial purchase contract is drafted and signed later, the agreements made in the preliminary contract are already legally binding and therefore leave little chance for subsequent negotiation.

In general, the following points should be considered with respect to these contracts:

See the results of the Due Diligence:

The results of the Due Diligence have to be included in the contract and known it by both parties. It is important to identify the owners, the property itself and any charges that may exist on it.

Who signs the preliminary contract?

Although less common today, these contracts may be signed by the estate agent on behalf of the seller. This practice should be avoided, because in case of dispute it is more difficult to verify if the act was with or without enough power of representation. If a person signs such contracts in Spain on behalf of another, enough authorization can only be demonstrated without questioning their veracity, by means of a power of attorney. In the presence of the seller, a copy of the identification or passport will be requested, which will be attached to the contract accordingly.

Who receives the initial payment?

At first, the initial payment should be made directly to the seller as part of the purchase price, but in some cases both the estate agents and the lawyers involved act as trustees. If payment is not made directly to the seller, this fact has to be in writing and approved by the buyer and seller.

If payment is directed to the seller's lawyer, the seller acts as trustee in most cases and, under the contract, holds the payment until the notary appointment. If the notarial sales contract is signed as agreed, the lawyer transmits the advance to the seller as part of the purchase price.

If the public deed of sale of the property does not materialize, the lawyer transmits it back to the buyer if the seller has mediated fault, or to the seller if the fault comes from the buyer.

Here it is crucial how the clauses are identified in the preliminary contract, because in only a few cases the loss of the deposit constitutes a true withdrawal right. In other cases, the other party, despite the loss of the advance, can legally seek compliance with the purchase contract. In addition, a certificate of bank ownership has to be attached with the account number specified in the contract.

How is the deposit made?

The initial payment should never be made in cash. If the payment is delivered to brokers or lawyers in this way, legally it must not exceed €1,000, so a cash payment is not appropriate here in any case.

In these cases of tax evasion, the purchase price that is actually paid is higher than the purchase price that is ultimately specified in the notarial purchase deed, so the seller has less taxable income from the sale.

However, this simulated purchase price not only affects the taxes that the seller need to pay, but is also used to calculate the taxes that the buyer has to pay (Property Transfer Tax, ITP or documented legal acts, AJD), which is why the buyer would also evade taxes.

Public deed signature:

The down payment contract has to specify the date scheduled for signature by the parties of the public deed of sale in the notary. Especially in so-called "purchase options", the responsibility to make the appointment is the buyer who must demonstrably inform the seller in writing of the notarized appointment. If the buyer does not inform the seller in time, the amounts delivered to the seller can be lost as a down payment on the purchase.

The difficulty of being able to test the notification in case of dispute, often prevents emails, phone calls, SMS, etc. be a suitable method. A certified letter in writing with acknowledgment of receipt and content certificate (Burofax) is usually the only solution to receive conclusive confirmation.

However, if an appointment is made directly in the contract and a notary is chosen to sign, this type of problem can be avoided, since both the seller and the buyer know exactly when and where to sign the public deed of purchase. Since the notary fees are primarily paid by the buyer, the buyer can freely choose the notary he trusts. If it is necessary that other people besides sellers and buyers appear in the notarial deed (lawyers, translators, authorized representatives, etc.), it is advisable to find a suitable appointment in advance and record it directly in the contract.

5. The notarial deed of purchase

For the purchase of the property to be registered in the Land Registry, it is necessary to conclude the purchase contract in the notary. For this purpose, a private purchase contract can be authenticated in the presence of both contracting parties, and the purchase contract can be added directly in a notarial deed.

Differences from the private purchase contract:

For the notary to be able to register a purchase contract, he is obliged to document all payments over €10,000. If the purchase is only processed in a private purchase contract, problems can arise quickly.

Another disadvantage of the private purchase contract, in case of dispute, is that there is no reliable evidence on the date and the signer. If the other contracting party denies that it signed the contract or that it was not signed on the mentioned date, in many cases it is necessary to commission a calligraphic expert test in Court, which often does not produce clear results. However, if the purchase contract is registered in front of the notary from the beginning, all signatories must identify themselves. The notary publicly certifies the identity of the signatories and their legal capacity.

Proof of payments:

To avoid fictitious purchases and money laundering, the notary is obliged to document in writing all transactions that exceed €10,000.

In most cases, payment of the remaining purchase price is made by bank check. The buyer's bank issues a money order to the seller, which is delivered to a notary. In this case, the notary will attach a copy of the check to the notarized deed of purchase to document the payment. Even if it is not common, payment can also be made directly by bank transfer.

Due to the stricter laws to prevent money laundering and various incidents in some law firms, direct payment between buyer and seller is clearly recommended today.

Bilingual contracts and sworn translators:

The skills of foreign buyers are often not enough to understand a sales contract that is only written in Spanish. Since the notarial deed of sale must always be written at least in Spanish, there are basically two ways to register it between the contracting parties with different languages:

a) Bilingual notaries:

If the Spanish notary also speaks a language other than Spanish, he may sign a bilingual contract, or he may reproduce the content directly in that language.

b) Sworn Translators or Interpreters:

The most used solution is to hire a translator or interpreter to go with you for the notarial appointment and translate the notary's statements into your native language. Even the translator may not necessarily has to be a sworn interpreter, it is strongly recommended that the translator has a recognized degree or be a bilingual legal expert (lawyer, authorized representative, etc.). It is also recommended that you review the contract in advance and clarify any questions before sign.

Notarial appointment:

In Spain, it is generally advisable to trust your lawyer when choosing a notary.

As soon as the notary has made copies of your identification cards and NIE certificates, they generally ask for your address, your marital status, profession and, if applicable, your marriage status.

In Spain, there are different marriage status:

- Community of property.
- Separation of property.
- Participation of property.

Once all the above information has been collected, the identity process of the parties involved begins by comparing the identity cards with the attached copies. Once all the parties have been identified, the notary reads the most important points of the purchase contract and, if necessary, provides certain information about the payment of the corresponding taxes. If an interpreter is included, he will translate the notarized deed of purchase in advance, as well as all instructions given verbally by the notary.

After reading the deed, everyone involved signs it and, if necessary, the bank check is delivered. Generally, you can pay the notary's fees directly in cash or by credit card and you will immediately receive a simple copy of the deed. With this simple copy, you can now add water and electricity.

Depending on the notary, the issuance of the original deed takes up to a week. You or your lawyer will be notified directly by the notary. If you received the original deed, you have to seal it by paying the tax.

6. Tax payment

The purchase of real estate in Spain is subject to the payment of taxes. The tax rate to be paid mainly depends on whether the property is purchased for primary or secondary residence, which is particularly important in the case of private purchases.

Property transfer tax (ITP) or Value added tax (VAT):

If we are dealing with a purchase of a newly built home, the seller or the property developer must always pay value added tax. However, if the property is not newly built but a second buyer, the tax that must be met is the property transfer tax.

If the seller is a legal entity or entrepreneur (for example, bought directly from a real estate company), it is also possible to pay value added tax, instead of the property transfer tax.

People subject to tax payment:

Property transfer tax is paid directly by the buyer and the value added tax by the seller. It be explicitly specified in the purchase contract that the seller is subject to value added tax, because only then the buyer can be sure that he does not have to pay the property transfer tax.

An important peculiarity when buying with value added tax is that the buyer is exempt from the property transfer tax, but not from the tax on legal documents acts and, therefore, must pay taxes in all cases.

If Value Added Tax is paid in this regard, the purchase is exempt from the Property Transfer Tax but is subject to the Tax on documented legal acts.

If the purchase is exempt from Value Added Tax and is therefore subject to Property Transfer Tax, the purchase is automatically exempt from the Tax on documented legal acts.

Tax rate and benefits:

Both the Property Transfer Tax and the Tax on Documented Legal acts are taxes payable to the Autonomous Communities, which are regulated and administered differently according to the autonomous region.

a) Property transfers tax: Generally, this tax ranges 8% for the first €300,000 of the value of the property. If the value of the property is greater than that amount, the tax rate increases to 10% (11% in Extremadura). Depending on each Autonomous Community, various tax expenses of up to 6% can be deducted. In most of the Communities, these tax deductions are based on the purchase for residential purposes or if you establish your permanent residence in the property in the following two years. You can check the current tax rates and applicable exemptions on the website of your Autonomous Community using the keywords "ITP" or "Tax on property transfers".

b) Value added tax and Tax on documented legal acts: If we are dealing with a new construction and first sale home, consequently, value added tax and tax on documented legal acts must be paid. The total tax rate ranges from 10% to 11.5% of the purchase price.

Property transfer tax (ITP) and value added tax (AJD) payment:

Both taxes are administered and taxed directly by the Autonomous Communities, and payment is made by filing the corresponding tax declaration. In most cases, taxes must be paid within 30 days after signing the notarial deed of purchase, because on the one hand it causes the transfer of property, and on the other hand it is a document taxed with the Tax on documented legal act. It should be noted that the calculation and presentation of the corresponding tax declaration in Spain is generally not carried out by the notary.

If the declaration is not made by the buyer himself, it is advisable to hire a tax advisor, or a lawyer specialized in buying properties.

Regarding the payment of the tax, this can be done in all the Autonomous Communities both personally and electronically. If the tax return is filed electronically, the amount can be made directly from your Spanish bank account.

Property transfer tax (ITP) in each Autonomous Community:

Depending on the Autonomous Community in which the property is acquired, the payment of the percentage established in the corresponding autonomous region has to be paid.

The percentage to be applied in our Autonomous Community is 8%, with except applying 3.5% to people who acquire the home for less than 130,000 euros, and use the property as a habitual residence, or not more of €180,000 for a person with a disability equal to or greater than 33%.

Aspects to know in the purchase of real estate by non-residents:

An important peculiarity is the purchase of real estate by non-residents in Spain. In these cases, the tax obligation is reversed, so the buyer is obliged to pay the increase of benefits and the tax on the increase in urban land value (IIVTNU) on behalf of the seller.

As it is a joint and several tax obligations, both the seller and the buyer are obliged to pay the taxes. If the seller does not pay the tax within the legal period, the Spanish Tax Agency can contact the seller and buyer directly. Sellers normally do not have other real estate in Spain and reside abroad.

To rule out later problems, it is recommended to ask sellers for a certificate of your tax residence. This certificate, issued by the Spanish tax office, can be attached to the notarial public deed, in which the sellers also ensure that they have their tax domicile in Spain at the time of purchase. If the seller has his tax residence abroad, this must be registered in the deed and the buyer must foresee the payment of the tax.

Therefore, the amount of this provision is retained directly by the buyer and paid directly to the tax office. If the seller insists on paying the tax himself, it is possible to attach the corresponding payment receipt to the notarized purchase contract to prove the payment of the tax.

7. Land Registry and Cadastre

After the tax payment, the corresponding Autonomous Community will stamp its public deed of purchase. The deed can only be registered in the Land Registry with this stamp.

Which Registry is competent?

There are different Land Registries in a city, in which case they bear the name of the city and a main number. You can find out which Land Registry office is competent to register your home by looking at the extract from the Land Registry, which can usually be found at the end of the notarial deed of purchase.

Registry structure:

The registers in Spain are basically ordered by the numbers of registered property. Each registered property has at least one sheet, which provides information on the description of the property and its owner. All property transfers, enrollments or deletions of mortgages, etc.

Important features of the Registry:

The transfer of ownership can generally only be requested by presenting the deed of purchase, so the processing time can be up to 2 months.

What documents are required?

To register the transfer of property in the Land Registry, it is generally necessary to present the notarized public deed stamped by the corresponding Autonomous Community. In some cases, the tax receipt will be sent directly from the Community to the corresponding Land Registry, which will allow registering in the future without presenting the original notarial deed of purchase.

How to avoid blocking in the Land Registry:

To avoid this registration block and therefore not depend on the seller's willingness to pay, it is possible to request the notary to send an electronic copy of the purchase certificate directly to the registry office. Even if many notaries already offer the transmission in a standard way, it is recommended to check if the transmission is mentioned in the notarial deed of purchase and if the notary has correctly sent the electronic copy after signing.

Completion and proof of ownership:

As soon as you receive the confirmation of registration from the Land Registry, you can request an extract directly in person or electronically on the website of the Spanish Land Registry, whose cost is approximately €10. With this extract electronically signed by the Registry, you can prove and assert your right against other administrations and individuals. The extract is also available in English for an additional fee and can be printed or sent electronically on a frequent basis by electronic signature.

Spanish Cadastre:

Spanish Cadastre is centrally administered by the Spanish cadastral office and is exclusively administrative in nature.

The registration form can be sent electronically with the electronic signature or can be made personally to the cadastral office. The corresponding model 901N can be completed on the web or downloaded from the Land Registry website.

When submitting with the electronic signature, the form must include the extract from the Land Registry and a copy of the certificates of the NIE numbers of the new owners, which can also be obtained electronically from the tax office.

III. OFF-PLAN SALE OR UNDER CONSTRUCTION

1. Introduction

Off-plan sale is a way of acquiring ownership of a property by signing a contract between a developer and a client. With this contract, the developer undertakes to deliver a home to the future buyer even when it is under construction.

The private sale contract contains the essential points by which the parties will be governed during the process. The developer must deliver a series of documentation so that the future buyer has the certainty that the future home is being built with all the legal guarantees.

This type of sale has a series of advantages, such as the possibility of accessing a completely new property, the agreement between the developer and the client to make some modifications to the specific property, or the possibility of paying the price in several installments throughout the Building process.

But as in any operation, there are also risks for buyers. During the process, the future owner of a home will pay out different amounts for the price, so it is necessary to take into account different aspects so that the money invested is not lost in the event that construction does not start or is not completed. complete within the agreed period, as agreed between the developer and the buyer.

In this sense, it is convenient to inform yourself in advance about the experience and reliability of the developer that will carry out the project, the land on which the future homes will be located, the existence of the appropriate construction permits, the price and method of payment and above all , that the money that will be disbursed is deposited in a special account that guarantees the return of it in case of any type of breach that involves the termination of the contract with the promoter.

With the legal reform of 2016 in this matter, the developer is obliged to contract an insurance or bank guarantee that ensures the amounts delivered by the buyers, and, as has been stated, the certainty that payments are made in a special bank account whose funds can be used exclusively for the construction of the property.

Legal guarantees that the promoter should provide:

- ✓ All payments are guaranteed by a bank through the appropriate guarantee.

- ✓ All payments are made to a special account opened for the construction of the property. If the property is not built, the buyer can demand the guarantee from the insurer.

One way of evaluating the possible risks in the purchase of a house of this type is through the **legal verification "Due-Diligence"** that must include at least the following points:

- ✓ Legal and economic analysis of the promoter (Mercantile register, representation, annual accounts, liquidity, etc.).

- ✓ Legal analysis of the property (Simple note, owners, real rights etc.).

- ✓ Work license, plans, quality memory, price, payment terms.

- ✓ Individualization protocol.

- ✓ Sales contract including the analysis of possible abusive clauses (choice of notary, deadlines, payments, etc.).

- ✓ Responsibility and guarantees of the promoter.

- ✓ Tax aspects.

2. Documents to check

If you want to buy a house that has not yet been built, a detailed study of all the documents provided by the developer must be carried out, to verify that there are no legal impediments that frustrate the completion of the project and delivery of your home.

A) Information from the Mercantile Registry:

The construction of real estate for sale can be carried out through a promoter or a construction cooperative.

The construction of real estate for sale can be carried out through a promoter or a construction cooperative. When the owner of the land is a developer, it is usually constituted as a Limited Company (S.L.). In practice, it is usual that the project of the houses that are being built or will be built in the future, is carried out by a developer.

Thanks to the Mercantile Registry, the buyer of the property can carry out a study on the trajectory and experience of the developer, making sure that it is constituted in accordance with the law, since all the information in the registry is public, it is advisable to request the information complete mercantile and latest annual accounts. Likewise, through a note from the commercial register it is possible to check who are the administrators, proxies and the registered office of the company.

B) Land Registry and building license:

Another aspect that must be verified by the buyer is the ownership of the land on which the future property is to be built. You have to go to the Property Registry to request a simple note, with which we can find out who is the owner of the land, its description, as well as if there are charges on the ownership that should be known by the buyer and if it is registered the new work, as well as contact the town hall to verify that the developer has the necessary licenses for the construction of the property. You can request a simple note through the link of the Registry provided in the previous section.

C) Plans, memory, price, and payment method:

The promoter must deliver the following documents to the buyer in order to verify by the latter that all the procedures are being carried out satisfactorily:

- House plans.
- Quality memories.
- Accessory services.
- Price.
- Way to pay.
- Description of the surface.

In the case of buying a property from a cooperative, the same documentation must be required, especially to verify urban licenses.

In this sense, when buying a new home under construction or

"off plan", the developer must provide the following information:

- ✓ Information from the Commercial Registry.
- ✓ General and detailed plans of the house.
- ✓ Instructions on the use and conservation of the facilities.
- ✓ A memory of the qualities.
- ✓ The total price and the form of payment.

In addition to these documents, it is also recommended to keep all those brochures where the developer has advertised the housing development, since they also link construction as if it were a contract.

D) Reservation contract, deposit contract, public deed and abusive clauses:

The purchase of a newly built home involves a series of contractual steps unknown to most of those involved.

a) Reservation contract:

With the reservation contract, the promoter guarantees the buyer the right to be able to buy a specific property, preventing the promoter from signing another reservation contract for the same property with another buyer. In general, this reservation is made effective with the disbursement of an amount that can amount, in relation to the total price of the property, to about € 6,000. Failure to comply with this agreement normally leads to the loss of the payment made. Among other points, the deposit contract usually stipulates the form of payment and a maximum term to sign the private contract of sale, so that at this moment the planning of the next steps must be considered (NIE, Mortgage etc.).

b) Private contract of sale:

Once the date stipulated in the reservation contract has arrived and the appropriate documentation verification (Due Diligence) has been carried out, the parties sign the private sale contract or deposit contract. Especially important: this document cannot be signed before the developer has the Building License.

Since, in most cases, buyers choose to finance part of the price through a mortgage on the new property, it must be considered that, upon signing this document, it is usual for the buyer to make a 10% outlay of the total price, making from this moment and until the signing of the public deed of sale another disbursement of 10%, so it is normal that you have disbursed 20% of the total purchase price up to this moment. The remaining 80% of the price are usually financially available by banks, although according to each bank the percentage of equity capital approved for finance may depend, among others, on whether the buyer buys for a habitual residence or not. In the event that one of the parties terminates the sale contract, a series of penalties are agreed for both, which are set out in this document.

The amounts that are delivered as "deposit" are part of the total price to pay. Therefore, at the time of signing the public deed of sale, what has already been delivered by the buyer, will be deducted from the total price.

In case of default by the buyer, he will lose the signal and in case of default by the seller, he must return the deposit in duplicates.

It is important that the earnest money is agreed as "penitential" since only then is there a right to resign with loss of the earnest money delivered.

A series of abusive clauses that the buyer may encounter when signing a private sale contract must be taken into account:

- Force the buyer to subrogate the developer's mortgage.
- Impose the payment of the capital gain to the buyer.
- Impose a specific notary on the buyer.
- Unilateral changes in the project and contracting of additional services.
- Lack of insurance or guarantee that ensures the return of payments.
- Failure to register the completion of the work in the registry before signing the deed of sale.
- Pass on to the buyer the costs of access to the general supplies of the house (water, electricity ...).
- Empower the seller to increase the agreed price.

c) Deed of sale:

The last step for the buyer to acquire possession of their home is by signing the public deed of sale, which means that the promotion has been carried out in a totally satisfactory way. At this time, the buyer and seller sign the sale by the promoter to the buyer before a notary, which already allows the latter to register their ownership in the Property Registry.

In the event that a buyer has applied for a mortgage to finance their home, the bank granting the loan will also attend the notarial appointment at this time, to sign the mortgage loan deed from this moment. It should be borne in mind that the loan application must be made prior to the notary appointment for the mortgage sale.

d) Tax aspects: VAT and ITP:

A peculiarity of the sale of a new home or a property that is transmitted for the first time since its construction is the fact that the transaction is subject to VAT.

In this case, the promoter, not the buyer, has to pay 10% VAT directly, receiving the amount as part of the purchase price. Since the buyer has to pay in this way 10% in taxes (part of the price), the operation is exempt from ITP (Tax on Patrimonial Transmissions). Now, although VAT is paid directly to the developer and the operation is exempt from the ITP, the buyer does have to present a tax return, in this case the self-assessment of the Tax on Documented Legal Acts (AJD). This tax, although of less incidence compared to the others, is usually forgotten in the calculations of the total expenses of the operations, so it can be an unwanted surprise once the sale is signed.

Like the ITP, the AJD is administered and imposed directly by the Autonomous Communities, and payment is made by filing the corresponding tax return. In most cases, taxes must be paid within 30 days after the signing of the Public Deed. Here it should also be noted that the calculation and presentation of the corresponding tax return, in Spain is generally not carried out by the notary.

IV. EXTERNAL FINANCING

1. Forms of financing your home

The purchase of real estate in Spain can be financed through national Spanish or foreign banks, although access to the latter has been hindered in practice by the new mortgage law.

In order to protect consumers from abusive practices, the new law provides, among other things, for the electronic transmission of conditions between the bank and the notary, which makes it necessary for the bank to use the digital platform enabled for this purpose. In practice, most foreign banks have yet to meet these new requirements, which makes it difficult to take out a mortgage with a foreign bank. aufdeutsch02

As in practice this option would normally only be advantageous for non-residents with residence and their own bank abroad, indirect financing is often avoided here, leaving an encumbered property and the loan amount is used to buy the Spanish property. In this case, the entire process is carried out abroad and the mortgage is also registered in the corresponding property registry in the foreign country.

The connection with Spain is only achieved by using the loan amount to directly buy a property at no charge. Therefore, there are no more provisions that must be observed in the notarial appointment in Spain.

For residents of Spain, financing through Spanish banks is usually advantageous, especially if the property to be financed is the future habitual residence. In this case, banks usually finance at least 80% of the market value and the consumer has the option of paying off the mortgage for free or changing banks at any time.

Documents normally required:

> 1. Simple Note from the Land Registry. It is usually provided by the seller or the real estate agent. If it is not available from them, an extract can be requested electronically at the registry headquarters.

> 2. Last declaration of income tax (IRPF). It should be noted here that most Spanish banks continue to recognize only income tax returns (IRPF) for valuation purposes. If you have lived in Spain for less than a year and have not yet submitted your income tax return, you

may be required to have the last return filed in the country of departure translated into Spanish.

3.   Payroll/Quarterly tax returns. If you work in Spain, it is usually enough to present the last 3 payrolls. If you are self-employed, the last 3 quarterly financial statements (forms 130 and 303) are normally required.

Steps to follow:

1.   Sign a private contract with the sellers with the right of withdrawal in case the mortgage is not granted.

2.   Consultation with the bank and presentation of the documents mentioned in the last section.

3.   Confirmation by the bank and drafting of internal documents in the branch.

4.   Election of a notary and electronic transmission of the conditions to the notary.

5.   Prior informative act of the conditions of the mortgage loan and drafting of the corresponding public deed.

6.   Appointment before a notary with the seller and the bank to sign the deed of sale and the mortgage deed.

(Note that at least 10 days must elapse between the receipt of the conditions by the notary and the date of signing the mortgage).

2. Expenses and taxes related to the signature.

According to the new mortgage law, the bank must bear almost all the costs related to the mortgage. In the case of a mortgage for the purchase of the habitual residence, the consumer only has to bear the expenses of the appraiser.

The bank has to pay all other expenses (notary, Land Registry, stamp, Agency). Since the purchase is usually signed at the same time as the mortgage, the Agency will continue to charge the associated costs. Regarding costs, the bank bears all the costs of the mortgage and the buyer bears all the costs of the purchase deed.

V. REAL PROPERTY

1. Fiscal aspects

Property in Spain carries tax obligations and consequences:

Property Tax (IBI):

The Property Tax is a tax imposed by municipalities on property, which is generally paid by all owners. The tax is paid annually or semi-annually, and the exact payment term depends on each municipality.

Authority responsible for the administration of the tax sends each year the corresponding payment receipt. Since the tax is payable, even if the receipt of payment cannot be delivered, it is advisable to grant the city government direct debit authorization. The amount of the tax depends on the cadastral value of the house. See the next section for more information.

If the property is sold, the seller is generally required to pay the tax throughout the year, even if the property changes hands at the beginning of the year. In practice, however, it often happens that the tax is shared between the buyer and the seller.

Community of goods:

If a property has multiple owners, they are jointly and severally liable to pay the tax. If the property is part of a community partnership, an undivided estate, or if you have multiple partners for other reasons, each partner can pay the tax and then request a refund from the others.

Personal Income Tax (IRPF):

In addition to the Property Tax payable at the level of each municipality, the property also has an impact on the income tax, corresponding tax at the state level. Personal Income tax is always paid if you have your main or tax residence in Spain. In this sense, the tax base depends on one of the following factors:

a) Primary residence (habitual residence): If you use your property as your primary residence, it is generally not subject to Personal Income Tax.

b) Property acquired and intended for rent (return on real estate capital): if you rent your property, income is taxed as income from real estate capital (return on real estate capital). If the property is rented for only part of the year (vacation home rental, short term rental), days not rented are subject to tax as their own use. In these cases, it should be noted that deductible expenses can only be attributed to the days rented. If the property is only rented for half the year, only half of the expenses can be deducted as a percentage.

It should be noted that this income is generally taxable by filing a quarterly tax return. For more information on rentals, see the corresponding chapter.

c) <u>Self-use (imputation of rent)</u>: The proper use of the property is always subject to tax if it is not the owner's primary residence or is rented. In this case, between 1% and 2% of the cadastral value is evaluated as taxable income, which is then taxed between 19% and 22%, like income from rentals and leases. With a cadastral value of €100,000, the income tax is around 190 euros per year, which is paid without applying any tax relief.

Income Tax on non-resident (IRNR):

If you have your tax residence abroad, you must tax the owner-occupant or the rental income, as the property is not used as your primary address. In this case, rental income is generally subject to tax first in Spain and then abroad. Tax paid in Spain can be deducted from the national tax declaration using the corresponding double taxation agreement.

2. Administrative Aspects

In addition to paying the corresponding taxes, the administrative aspects of buying a home must also be considered in Spain. These administrative aspects are generally related to the classification of the land, the possibility of building on them, the construction restrictions and the determination of the value of the property to calculate the taxes to pay.

Cadastre Update:

As already mentioned in the previous chapter, the Spanish cadastral office is an administrative registry that, unlike Lands Registries, is managed centrally. However, the data from the cadastre office have no effect on the property or on the registered charges.

Even if this data may seem less important than the Land Registry, it is important regarding the size of the property, as well as in terms of the use and size of individual buildings, to keep this data updated whenever changes occur, since that these are used to calculate the property tax. All owners are required to report any changes immediately. If real estate data is not provided in the correct way, tax evasion may be possible.

The cadastral value is made up of the value of the land, the value of the buildings and the type of buildings.

Conversions, additions and renewals:

Before making conversions, additions, or renovations to the property, you should verify the construction plans and local building regulations.

In Spain, a building permit must be applied for in advance for almost all construction projects (building permit), which in many cases has been replaced by a prior "responsible declaration". In the case of the responsible declaration, it is enough to present it before the start of construction without having to wait for approval.

Even if smaller building permits can be applied for, larger conversions, additions or renovations require a corresponding construction plan, always drawn up by an architect or civil engineer (rigger). The latter generally requests appropriate approval.

Check the construction restrictions:

In the past, especially in coastal areas and especially in rural areas, many properties were built on undeveloped land. Even if this led to the demolition of the property in some serious cases, most of these properties could remain with a construction restriction. There are far-reaching construction restrictions on these properties, which are built outside urban planning legality, some of which not only prohibit additions or extensions, but may even prohibit renovations. Even if the seller must expressly state this fact, if in doubt, a structural report from the city government should be obtained. Even if the property is trouble-free and complies with applicable law, local building regulations may have to be observed. In urban areas it may happen that it is not possible to exceed a certain height or number of floors, that the property or facade is a protected building, or in rural areas, additions that are not used for agricultural purposes are prohibited or that other buildings do not are used for residential purposes.

3. Sale of Spanish real estate

When selling real estate in Spain, the tax aspects that such transaction entails must be considered. To do this, read carefully the following.

Tax consequences for the seller and exemptions:

The taxes paid to sell a property are:

- Personal Income Tax, only tax the capital gain from said sale. In other words, basically, only the difference between the sale price and the purchase price will be taxed. If this difference is positive, you must pay the taxes related to that amount. On the contrary, if the difference is negative, it means that you will have incurred losses. In this case, you can deduct these losses on your return.

- Property Tax is not paid when selling the apartment. It is paid annually and must be paid by the owner on January 1. However, when selling an apartment, you can pass on the proportional part of Property Tax to the buyer.

- Tax on the Increase in Urban Land Value is the second of the taxes for the sale of housing. Better known as capital gain, this tax is applied to the increase in the value of the land from the moment of purchase to the moment of its sale. This is a municipal tax, and the final amount to be paid depends on the cadastral value of the home, the years you have owned it, and the town where your home is located.

When selling a house, the first tax that we must be considered is the Personal Income Tax.

To pay it, follow this procedure:

1. The sale of the property is made in a notary and Land Registry. In this way, the sale is implemented in a public document.

2. When filing the income statement, all the data related to the sale will already be included in the form to be completed.

3. It must be checked that all the information is correct.

Only if the property is sold for more money than we bought it at the time sale has supposed a patrimonial profit, would have to pay the personal income tax. To calculate the capital gain, all the expenses derived from selling the house, possible reforms, etc. have be considered. Once we know what we have earned by selling a house, the income tax will only be applied to the part on which a profit has been obtained. For example, if a house is bought for €100,000 (expenses included), a reform of €10,000 is made and it is sold for €150,000 (expenses included), we will have obtained a capital gain of €40,000. Consequently, income tax will only be paid for those €40,000.

In any case, the income tax that is applied is as follows:

- 19%: In earnings of up to €6,000.

- 21% In earnings from €6,000 to €50,000.

- 23%: In earnings over €50,000.

Luckily, it is not always necessary to pay in the personal income tax the capital gain obtained with the sale of a property, since there are exceptions to the general rule that are the following:

- Reinvestment of habitual residence. If you sell your usual home to buy another, you will not have to pay the rent for the capital gain. In addition, you have a period of two years to reinvest.

- People over 65 who sell their habitual residence. In this case, there is no additional requirement to apply the exemption.

- People over 65 years of age who use the profit to contract an annuity. If the house sold is not the habitual residence, you can avoid paying taxes if you use that money to contract an annuity.

In the rest of cases, it will be necessary to pay in the Personal Income Tax and for this it is essential to know the taxation for capital gains in the sale of real estate 2020.

Non-resident seller: In the sale of a property located in Spain by a person residing abroad, before going to the notary, you should know that the taxes that correspond to the seller in that transmission, will have to be paid into the Public Treasury. Therefore, the buyer of the home must retain the seller 3% of the sale price at the time of signing the public deed of sale in the notary. And this is so because in every purchase and sale of real estate, the seller will be obliged to pay tax on the capital gain obtained as a result of the transfer. Tax legislation establishes the rules for calculating this profit, which will generally be determined by the difference between the transmission and acquisition values. But when the seller is non-resident in Spanish territory, to ensure the collection of the tax, the law foresees that the buyer will retain 3% of the purchase price and make the deposit on account of that amount before the State Tax Administration Agency. Generally, this 3% is discounted at the time of formalizing the checks that the buyer delivers to the seller at the notary when signing the public deed.

Subsequently, the transferor will have to carry out the declaration and the payment of the final tax. As a result, the Tax Administration will return, if applicable, the remaining part of the amount retained and entered by the buyer. All this in the terms and in the manner indicated in the Law and the Regulation of the Income Tax on Non-residents where the consequences of non-compliance with this obligation are also established.

If the transferor accredits with a certificate issued by the competent Tax Administration, which is not subject to that tax, the withholding and deposit on account to which we have referred will not proceed. This will happen if the transferor is subject to Personal Income Tax (IRPF) or Corporate Income Tax (IS). In these cases, the checks delivered to the notary will cover the entire price of the operation.

Non-Resident Income Tax; Model 210 (seller) and model 211 (buyer):

Model 210 will be filed with the Agency Tax and applies to Income Tax on Non-Resident whether they are natural or legal persons. It also extends to foreigners residing in Spain for labor reasons, as well as to entities in attribution of income established abroad with presence in Spanish territory. It is important to note that, if you reside outside of Spain, but a relation of benefits is maintained for the income obtained from the rental or sale of properties that are located within Spanish territory, the presentation of Model 210 must be effective.

Regarding the term of presentation of model 210 when an amount is due to be paid, the following rules need to be considered:

- The imputed income from urban properties must be declared during the calendar year following the accrual date.

- Income derived from transfers of real estate: three months after the expiration of one month from the date of the transfer of the property.

- Rest of income: the first twenty calendar days of the months of April, July, October and January, in relation to income whose accrual date is included in the previous calendar quarter.

Regarding the deadline for filing model 210 requesting the return of amounts withheld, the following rules need to be considered:

- Income derived from transfers of real estate: within three months after the expiration of one month from the date of the transfer of the real property.

- Rest of income: from February 1 of the year following the accrual of the declared income and within a period of four years counted from the end of the declaration period and withholding income.

Model 211 will be presented to the Agency Tax by the person obliged to retain or enter an account (acquirer, natural or legal person, resident or non-resident) in the acquisition of real estate from non-residents without permanent establishment within a period of one month from the date of transmission.

Once the deposit has been made, he will deliver the "copy for the non-resident transferor" of the Model 211 itself to that person, who will use it in order to justify the payment on account when he submits self-assessment for the income derived from the transmission, and will keep it in his be able to have the "copy for the acquirer" as proof of the income made.

Update of the Land Registry and Cadastre:

Even if the buyer requests the transfer of property in the Land Registry and the Cadastral office, it is advisable to check both registries after a few months to determine if the changes have been made correctly. This is particularly important with respect to the cadastral office, since in the absence of a new registration, requests for payment of real estate tax will continue to be issued in your name.

.

VI. RENTAL

1. Renting your Spanish real estate

In Spain, a basic distinction is made between rentals for tourist purposes (periods of up to 2 months per tenant) and long-term rentals.

If the same person rents the property for more than two months, a distinction must be made in this long-term rental, between the apartment rental and the non-apartment rental, so the rental law only protects the rental of previous apartments. However, if you rent for commercial purposes, or if the tenant intends to carry out a commercial activity in the building, this does not necessarily count as renting the apartment and the contract is governed solely by the will of the contract. Here it is important that the cause of non-rent is recorded in the rental agreement (commercial premises, shops, etc.).

The difference between apartment rentals and non-apartment rentals is mainly the legal regulation of both types of contracts and the taxes to pay.

In the case of renting an apartment, all contractual clauses that put the tenant at a disadvantage compared to legal regulations are void and are considered not established. In addition, the binding legal regulations also apply to furniture, parking spaces, garage spaces or other objects. However, in the area of non-apartment rentals, most legal provisions can be excluded by the will to contract.

Regarding the taxes to be paid, rental income will be taxed quarterly by filing the corresponding tax returns on both apartment rentals and non-apartment rentals. This applies to residents or owners based in Spain, as well as non-residents.

If you rent your property for non-residential purposes, the rental price always includes sales tax, which you, as the owner, must also pay to the tax office on a quarterly basis.

Rental price and payment:

The rental price is freely negotiable. Unless otherwise stated in the contract, it must be paid to the owner monthly within the first 7 days. If payment is not made by bank transfer and is delivered to the owner in cash, the landlord is required to provide the tenant with a receipt as proof of payment.

Increases in the rental price during the contract period can only be made at the end of each year and only if expressly provided for in the contract.

These regulations may be contractually amended or excluded for non-apartment rentals.

Rental period and automatic renewal:

Royal Decree-Law 7/2019, of March 1, establishes that if the duration of the lease is less than five years, or less than seven years if the owner is a legal entity, once the contract expires, it will be extended mandatory for annual terms until the lease reaches a minimum duration of five years, or seven years if the owner is a legal entity, unless the lessee confirmed to the lessor, at least thirty days before the date of termination of the contract or of any of the extensions, your will not to renew it.

If the expiration date of the contract, or any of its extensions, arrives, once at least five years have elapsed, or seven years if the owner is a legal entity, neither party was entitled to the other, at least Four months before that date in the case of the lessor and at least two months in advance in the case of the lessee, his will not to renew it, the contract will be compulsorily extended for annual periods up to a maximum of three more years, except that the lessee forget the landlord one month before the termination date of any of the annuities, his will not to renew the contract.

Cancellation before the end of the agreed rental period:

If the apartment is rented, the tenant can terminate the lease at any time after the first 6 months, even if several years of rental have been agreed in the lease.

Both a 30-day notice period and any compensation stipulated in the rental agreement must be observed. If the compensation for early termination was agreed in the contract, in no case may it exceed a monthly rent per year of pending rent.

Example: If the tenant pays a monthly rent of €400 and wants to end the lease 1.5 years before the agreed rental period, he pays a maximum of €600 in compensation. If you want to end the contract before the first 6 months, the remaining months must be paid in full until the first 6 months are reached.

Electricity, water, community expenses and other expenses:

Maintenance costs, community, taxes, etc. they must always be paid by the homeowner. If these expenses are not included in the rental agreement, they are included in the rental price. For the tenant to bear these costs, an explicit mention of this must be made in the lease. In practice, both taxes and community fees are already included in the rental price. Electricity, water, gas, telephone and all other costs directly caused by the tenant are normally borne by the tenant.

Deposit and guarantee:

When entering into an apartment rental agreement, it is mandatory to agree on a deposit whose amount corresponds to a monthly rent. If the deposit is returned to the tenant within the month following the end of the contract or the return of the keys, no interest is paid. It is up to the contracting parties to decide whether additional guarantees will be concluded.

Assignment of contracts and subletting:

The tenant can only assign the lease to a third person if the owner has given his express written consent. To sublet part of the apartment, the tenant also requires the prior consent of the landlord. When the lease ends, the sublet also ends automatically.

Repairs and maintenance:

Furniture, washing machine, kettle, fridge, television, etc.

Most of the Spanish apartments are rented partially furnished, and certain appliances such as the washing machine or the fridge are often part of the furniture. Under the current Leasing Law, the homeowner must make or pay for all repairs if necessary, to maintain proper housing conditions. If such appliances and furniture have been used diligently by the tenant, the landlord must repair or replace them with others if necessary. But if the damage is caused by faulty or negligent behavior of the tenant, it will bear the costs of repair. It should be noted that the lessee is responsible for the annual maintenance of the gas boilers, etc., and any malfunction or damage to the devices must be reported immediately and as quickly as possible to the owner.

Water pipes, taps, paint, etc.

The same applies here too: the tenant must bear negligent or negligent damages. If there is wear, the owner is responsible.

Minor repairs

The tenant is responsible for minor repairs, normal cleaning and maintenance of the devices, replacement of light bulbs, etc.

Early termination by the tenant:

If the owner sells the rental property to a buyer in good faith, the buyer is not required to assume the rental agreement. To avoid premature termination of the lease for sale, the lease can be registered in the Land Registry. In this way, the buyer is informed about the lease and is obliged to respect the lease.

It should be noted that in some regions of Spain (for example, País Vasco, Cataluña) there may be deviations from the aforementioned regulations, since they have an independent and local law, the so-called provincial law.

2. Vacation apartment rental

The reform to the apartment rental law in March 2013 allowed the Autonomous Communities to enact their own laws for the rental of vacation apartments, since from this moment they were excluded from the normal rental law. This new competence was used by all the Communities and it requires the owner to register the contract in the corresponding registry. As the requirements vary from one community to another, this chapter considers them according to the legal situation in Andalusia, with the Andalusian Government being the competent in this matter. Decree 28/2016 of February 2, on vacation apartments in Andalusia is applicable when you want to rent a home located in the Autonomous Community of Andalusia. The following cases are exempt from this law, in which other special laws apply and the requirements, registration and obligations differ in part from those described here:

1. The free provision of apartments.

2. Apartments rented by the same consumer for more than two months.

3. Rural holiday homes that fall within the scope of Decree 20/2002, of January 29, on rural or active tourism.

4. Holiday apartments that fall within the scope of Decree 194/2010, of April 20, on holiday apartments.

Therefore, it is particularly important from the outset to make a precise distinction about the house or property to be rented, that is, whether it is a question of holiday apartments, rural holiday houses or normal apartments.

Prerequisite for renting vacation apartments:

- Occupancy Certificate (first occupation license).

- Windows outside or in the garden and the possibility of darkening them. * *

- Rooms must display furniture and electrical equipment necessary for immediate use.

- Air conditioning, if you want to rent from May to September and heating, if you rent from October to April. * *

- First-aid kit.

- Written tourist information (also digitally possible) on various aspects of the area: leisure activities, shops, supermarkets, public transport, the nearest emergency room, city map, etc.

- Complaint sheet and signs clearly visible.

- Basic cleaning.

- Household items and two pairs of bedding.

- Telephone number to deal with possible problems

immediately.

- Information on the use of household appliances.

- Information on the correct use of the devices, restrictions on pets or smoking.

* Compliance with these requirements is not mandatory if the rented property is a listed building or a building of cultural interest.

Presentation of the declaration of receipt of the license:

Before renting a property, and in any case before its announcement, it is necessary to present a statement to the Andalusian Government, confirming that the property meets the relevant conditions for renting holiday apartments.

Once the declaration has been sent, the apartment will be assigned a corresponding number, which must be indicated in all advertisements and on all websites.

Form of the lease:

Each client must receive a written rental agreement, specifying at least the vacation apartment number, owner's name, tenant's name, as well as the price and rental period. In addition, the owner's phone number must be registered in the contract. The tenants must facilitate their identity document or passport so that the owner can make the corresponding notification and the necessary registration of the travelers. The retention period for all contracts is at least one year.

Traveler registration book:

An important feature of renting holiday apartments is the obligation to register travelers (traveler registration sheet) and transmit this information to the responsible Police or Guard Civil within 24 hours. The owner must transmit the data of his clients to the Police. It should be noted that the corresponding form must be completed by all clients over the age of 16 and, in any case, must include the following information: identification number, validity, name, sex, date of birth, date of arrival, nationality and the vacation apartment number. The relevant forms are collected in a folder and the data is transmitted to the responsible police within 24 hours.

Even if they can be delivered personally to the Police, transmission by fax or through the corresponding website is clearly recommended. For online streaming, the police only need to register once.

Other important aspects regarding the price:

The price offered must be the final price:

- ✓ Water, electricity and cleaning before arrival, as well as bedding, must always be included in the price.

- ✓ Important restrictions regarding payment, reservation and the right of cancellation must be observed, these must be considered.

- ✓ If additional services are offered that are similar to the area of activity of the hotels, for example, restaurant, hospitality, regular cleaning of rooms, etc., the corresponding VAT must be paid, which must be shown on the invoices and paid by the owner.

✓ The periods used by the owner can be taxed on the corresponding tax return under "income allocation". If you are thinking of renting your apartment, it is always advisable to know in advance the necessary administrative acts, for example if the property is located in rural areas more than 500 meters from the beach, you may need to request other licenses.

Disadvantages of vacation rental:

In the Balearic Island and in other cities such as Barcelona, excessive rental of holiday apartments has caused social unrest among the population, which has led to increased controls and the imposition of fines. However, in practice these controls are mainly directed against illegal vacation rental houses that do not obtain the corresponding license, as well as Internet providers that continue to advertise or mediate unregistered holiday homes on their portals. To avoid problems, all legal requirements must be met, and the apartment must be registered with the corresponding Autonomous Community Administration, in Andalusia, the Andalusian Government. For rentals that do not comply with legal requirements, fines of between €20,000 and 40,000 are established.

VI. RESIDENCE IN SPAIN

1. Primary or secondary residence

The place of residence is basically the same as the "Tax residence". If you reside in Spain, you are considered "resident" for administrative and tax purposes. Unlike administrative residence, tax residence has much broader consequences, since as soon as you are a tax resident, you must tax your worldwide income in Spain and comply with the corresponding tax obligations (Tax returns, model 720). In this sense, as a natural person in accordance with article 9 of the Spanish Personal Income Tax Law, you are not only a resident in Spain if you are in Spain for 183 days a year, but also if you have a permanent residence in Spain (Property or rent) or if you have the center of your life interests in Spain.

a)   183 days a year in Spain:

Even if a permanent stay in Spain is at first sight the easiest way to determine your place of residence, it is almost impossible for the Spanish Tax Agency to prove this condition due to the absence of border controls.

b)   Permanent residence in Spain:

If a person has their permanent place of residence in Spain (primary or secondary residence), and the Spanish Tax Agency suspects this, and even if it is their second home for less than 183 days, electricity and water bills, telephone bills, etc. they may be enough to assume that the tax residence is in Spain.

c)   The center of your main interests:

This last condition can generally only be confirmed by speculation when suspecting that the taxpayer is domiciled in Spain if his or her non-separated spouse and minor children are domiciled in Spain using the above criteria.

2. Non-resident tax

Real estate plays an important role here, as it is linked to both Property tax and Personal Income tax. In order to carry out administrative acts in the corresponding tax offices, you need the Identification Number in any case. If you already have the NIE, this is also your tax number. If you do not have a NIE yet, you can request the number directly from the Tax Agency.

1) Property Tax (IBI):

As discussed in previous chapters, this property tax is applied. If you have multiple properties or properties in different municipalities, the tax return must be filed separately in each municipality. Basically, the amount to be paid depends on the cadastral value and the Autonomous Community in which it is located.

In general, the payment can be domiciled by providing the account number in which you want the charge to be made by the corresponding Administration. If the direct debit procedure is not approved, the exact payment date must be observed by respective municipality, which is generally between September and November.

2) Income Tax on Non-resident (IRNR):

a) <u>Own use:</u>

Taxable income is generally one to two percent of the cadastral value.

In this case, the property is assessed as an increase in assets and therefore you must pay taxes, even if you use the property as a second home yourself.

b) <u>Income from the rental of real estate:</u>

It should be noted here that owners who have their tax domicile in Germany, Austria or Switzerland can deduct certain expenses from the tax because the same expenses can be deducted that apply to people residing in Spain. The tax expires quarterly, which means that the corresponding tax return must be filed within the first 20 days of January, April, June, and October. You can find more information about deadlines, forms and special features on the website of the Tax Agency.

c) <u>Income from the sale of real estate:</u>

When selling real estate, the difference between the value at the time of purchase and the sale value must be taxed, since in most cases this represents an increase in assets.

There are several and extensive tax exemptions. In case you invest the product directly in another property that later becomes your main residence or for people over 65 years of age.

It should be noted that the hypothetical increase in assets should also be taxed with donations. If you donate property, the gift recipient must not only pay the gift tax but must also tax the value of the property as an increase in assets.

3) Wealth Tax (IP)

The Wealth Tax was reinstated for a limited period for the fiscal years 2011 to 2017, with the first net assets of €700,000 free tax, having to file an estate tax return if this net worth is greater than €700,000 or if the gross assets (without deduction of liabilities) are greater than €2 million.

4) Inheritance Tax (IS):

Inheritance Tax is the responsibility of the Autonomous Communities, which apply exemption tax that fluctuate widely depending on the autonomous region. For example, in Madrid there is a 99.9% reduction in taxes, so there would be practically no amount to be paid in the processing of an inheritance, while in Murcia there are few and small exemptions in relation to the state tax rate. In the case of non-residents, it is easy to determine which tax law would be applied. This always applies if the heirs and testators have their tax domicile abroad. In this case, the rules of the Autonomous Community in which the property is located must apply to properties located in Spain. In the area of inheritances and testaments, it is advisable to know the tax advantages at an early stage.

5) Property Tax (IBI), VAT (IVA) and Legal Documents Acts Tax (AJD):

These taxes generally apply when buying property and must be paid by both residents and non-residents.

3. Tax residents

"Residents" of a Member State or another country residing in Spain, receive the same treatment as Spaniards in tax matters, since the main thing in tax matters is not their nationality but their place of residence. So, when living in Spain, there are the same rights and obligations as for all other places. In Spain, taxes are generally collected both by the state, by the Autonomous Communities and by the municipalities. Without going into more detail, the most important taxes can be summarized as follows:

1) Personal income tax (IRPF):

Statements made in the Non-Residents section apply here, so it should be noted that in this case the primary residence exemption may apply if the property is used accordingly, as the primary residence. If the property is not used as a primary residence, the following provisions apply:

a) Own use:

In this case, the property is assessed as an increase in assets, and therefore you must pay taxes.

b) Income from the rental of real estate:

It should be noted here that owners who have their tax domicile in Germany, Austria or Switzerland can deduct certain expenses from the tax because the same expenses that apply to people residing in Spain can be deducted. The tax expires quarterly, which means that the corresponding tax return must be filed within the first 20 days of January, April, June, and October. You can find more information about deadlines, forms and special features on the website of the tax office.

c) Income from the sale of real estate:

When selling real estate, the difference between the purchase value and the sale value should be taxed, since in most cases this represents an increase in assets.

There are several and extensive tax exemptions. In case you invest the product directly in another property that later becomes your main residence or for people over 65 years of age.

It should be noted that the hypothetical increase in assets should also be taxed with donations. If you give a property away, the gift recipient not only has to pay the gift tax but must also tax the value added of the property as an increase in assets.

2) Wealth Tax (IP):

Residents also must pay Wealth Tax on net assets of 700,000 euros. You must file an estate tax return if this net worth is more than 700,000 euros or if your gross equity (without deducting liabilities) is more than 2 million euros.

3) Inheritance and Gift Tax (ISD):

Inheritance tax is the responsibility of the Autonomous Communities, which, depending on the Community, apply a highly variable tax relief. In Madrid, thanks to a 99.9% reduction in taxes, there is practically no Inheritance Tax, while in Murcia there are few and small exemptions to apply to the state tax rate. The applicable tax law depends mainly on whether the heirs themselves live in Spain, if the testator was a tax resident in Spain and, in the case of real estate, where the property is located. If the testator has his main residence in Spain, the dispositions of the corresponding Autonomous Community will apply. In the area of inheritance and testaments, it is advisable to learn about tax advantages at an early stage and, if necessary, prepare tax planning under the inheritance law.

4) Property Tax (IBI), VAT (IVA) and Legal Documents Acts Tax (AJD):

As explained in the previous chapters, these taxes are generally incurred when purchasing property and must be paid by both residents and non-residents.

5) Property Tax (IBI):

It is paid regardless of whether the main residence is in Spain or not. Since the tax is paid annually to the municipalities, it is advisable to issue a direct debit authorization.

6) Circulation Tax and Vehicle Technical Inspection (ITV):

As soon as you permanently reside in Spain, it is also necessary to register or re-register your vehicle in Spain. If your vehicle is registered in Spain, you must pay the road tax to the municipality of your place of residence. Appropriate vehicle approval by the Vehicle Technical Inspection is also required.

4. Consequences of residence

In addition to the tax consequences, two other consequences of the main residence in Spain stand out: Model 720 and the need to choose the desired inheritance right.

A) Model 720:

People residing in Spain have been reporting their assets abroad since 2012. The obligation to provide information must be fulfilled by filing a return, separate from the tax return and can lead to exceptionally high fines if the exemption limit Legal is not presented or exceeded. The information obligation basically includes three areas:

1. Foreign bank accounts with a balance of more than €50,000:

With bank accounts, it should be noted that not only does the balance as of December 31 of the previous year play an important role, but the average balance for the last fiscal year must also be calculated. If one of the two values exceed the limit of €50,000, this aspect must be reported. Accounts opened in the same fiscal year and closed before December 31 are an exception. It is not necessary to register these accounts because they no longer exist on December 31. Regarding the duty to pay, it should be noted that this applies not only to the owner, but also to all authorized representatives.

2. Securities, shares, investments, company shares, insurance, pension claims over €50,000.00:

This should be reported if the total amount of all the mentioned assets exceeds the limit €50,000. If there is only life insurance worth €30,000 and shares worth €10,000, you generally should not report it.

3. Real estate abroad or rights over it for a value of more than €50,000:

In addition to simple real estate, this area also includes all real property rights (Purchase or usufruct options). Regarding the value of the property, it must be considered that both the value at December 31 and the acquisition value and that, in the case of partial or shared ownership, it is not the real participation, but the total value of the ownership what is decisive. This is particularly important in the case of a community property, because here both spouses must provide information on the total value if it exceeds the limit of €50,000.

Even if each of these three areas forms a separate obligation to provide information, it is recorded in a single document, tax model 720. It should be noted here that information should only be provided on areas that exceed the exemption limit. Example: if a person is a resident in Spain for tax purposes, owns a property in Germany worth €65,000 and has €40,000 in his German savings account, he only has to report his property, as this exceeds the limit of €50,000, but not on the German bank account.

Place, term and form of presentation of the declaration:

The declaration will generally be filed between February and May of the previous year and can only be sent electronically to the Tax Agency.

All areas are summarized in the same way, with which only a single document must be submitted (model 720). Since the return cannot be filed directly with the local tax office, but must be transmitted electronically, you need the electronic signature, which must be requested in advance. For more information on electronic signatures, see the corresponding chapter.

If you have already filed the declaration in the previous year, a new declaration is only necessary if there is an increase in assets of more than €20,000 in one of the three areas mentioned or if an area that has not yet been declared exceeds the limit of €50,000 for the first time and is therefore subject to declaration. It is also necessary to renew the declaration if an area or subarea that has already been explained is eliminated (closing an account, changing insurance, selling shares, etc.).

Fines for non-compliance:

Special attention should be paid to unusually high fines for non-compliance, failure to file the ordinary tax return. In case of non-presentation or incorrect presentation, a fine of at least €10,000 per area (€30,000) must be paid. A late declaration must be paid at least €1,500 per area. However, the amount of this fine appears to be small compared to the indirect fine payment established in Article 39.2 of the Personal Income Tax Law, since this article stipulates that all assets declared incorrectly are classified as investment income unjustified and counted for the oldest fiscal year without prescription. Given that all undeclared assets are counted as investment income for a single fiscal year, it is highly likely that the maximum tax rate will be applied and that the premature lien could generate a tax burden of up to 52% of the asset without occurring real investment income.

Even if in some cases half of the undeclared assets must be paid in Personal Income Tax, the Law of this tax establishes a catalog of fines for cases of suspicious or unjustified income. Currently, the additional fine for this corresponds to 150% of the total income tax obligation. The payment of additional taxes with an income tax rate of 52% plus the fine of 150% of the total tax obligation may, paradoxically, lead to the amount to be paid in the Tax Agency exceeding the value of the assets.

Refute the presumption of investment income:

The presumption of unjustified investment income can be rebutted for two reasons:

a) Assets correspond to income already taxed.

b) It can be shown that the assets correspond to income from fiscal years in which the taxpayer was not resident in Spain or was resident in another country.

Evaluation and recommendation:

Due to the increasing exchange of information on data and tax assets within the EU, the severity of the fines has been widely criticized by many. The very fact that the fines are calculated as a flat-rate and, at the same time, are significantly higher than the comparable ones in the area of tax returns, raises considerable legal questions about whether they are constitutional and comply with EU law.

It is highly recommended complying with the obligation of detailed information and, in case of doubt, if the assignments are reached, deliver a model 720 as a precaution to avoid possible drastic fines.

The practice; special cases:

- Spouse: it should be noted that each of the two spouses must provide information on the total value of the common assets if this exceeds the limit of €50,000 in the respective areas. Therefore, both spouses must provide information on a shared property worth €60,000 or a shared account with a balance of €70,000, even though the corresponding part is below the limit of €50,000.

- Short-term property: it is not necessary to be informed about the assets acquired and sold in the same fiscal year, since the obligation to declare only includes the assets that exist on December 31 of the fiscal year.

- Cash, jewelry, cars, boats, etc.: Basically, there is no obligation to provide information.

The new choice of European heritage in Spain:

Until August 2015, the inheritances of Europeans living in Spain were basically resolved in accordance with the law of their country. With the reform of the European inheritance law that came into force in August 2015, people from Member States now also inherit under Spanish law if the right to choose a law is not used in the testaments. The new Regulation of the European Succession Law 650/2012 covers both the principle of residence and the choice of law in European inheritance law. The new regulation applies to all cases of cross-border inheritance within the European Union in which the testator died after August 17, 2015. The only exceptions are Denmark, Ireland and the United Kingdom. In such cases, the relevant agreements between the EU and these countries will continue to apply. Cross-border inheritance cases are all those in which a person dies in a country other than their nationality in which they had their habitual residence.

Applicable law and choice of law:

According to article 21, it establishes that the state law of the last place of residence (habitual residence) of the testator will apply. The national law of the deceased is no longer automatically applied.

If a European citizen had already lived in Spain for 10, 20 or 30 years, the law of his country applied to succession until the reform of the inheritance law, without the latter being able to choose the law. But this regulation changed with some exceptions, the law now applies to the place of residence, since according to the regulation this "shows a particularly close and firm connection with the country in question."

Even if, in this regard, a "general assessment of the circumstances of the testator's life must be carried out in the years prior to his death, as well as at the time of his death and all relevant facts must be taken into account", a measure that may be sufficient to justify residence in Spain.

However, given that the link with the Spanish state, for European citizens living in Spain for only one year or for 30 or 40 years, may be very different, the new regulation provides for a choice of law through which the testator can be explicit when deciding which law to apply to your inheritance. Anyone who moves to Spain or who has been living in Spain for a longer period, but who still wants the inheritance law of their country to apply, can choose the corresponding law in the testament.

"The choice of law must be made explicitly in a statement in the form of a court order or as a result of the terms of that court order." If the testator has not made an express choice but has referred to specific provisions of a law, this is considered a valid choice of law.

To avoid possible problems with the interpretation of the last testament and offer the heirs the greatest possible legal certainty, it is strongly recommended choosing an explicit law.

Example of choice of law:

a) Walter moved to Spain upon receiving his pension in 1990 and died there in 2016 without a testament: due to the lack of choice of law, Spanish law must apply because Walter was a resident of Spain.

b) Paul moves to Spain upon receiving his pension in 2005 and dies there in 2016. Before his death, Paul renounces a Spanish testament expressly stipulating the application of the German inheritance law: the German inheritance law is it applies because Paul explicitly stipulated the application of his national law in his will.

Jurisdiction and jurisdiction agreement:

In principle, the Spanish courts are responsible for all assets if the testator had his habitual residence in Spain at the time of his death. However, if the testator chooses a different law from another country, it is possible to liquidate the entire estate before the courts of that country if the parties compromise with the courts of the place in question in the form of a court choice agreement or if the Spanish court applies to one of the Contracting Parties declared not responsible.

Hibernation problems in Spain:

To determine the testator's habitual residence or place of residence, the succession authority must make a general assessment of the circumstances of the testator's life in the years prior to his death and at the time of his death, taking into account all relevant facts, in particular the duration and regularity of the stay.

For example. If you stay in Germany for more than half the year and only spend part of the year in Spain (wintering), your place of residence will still be in Germany. However, if you live in Spain for more than half the year and are therefore resident for tax purposes in Spain, the aforementioned legal choice should always be made to avoid possible ambiguities.

CONCLUSION

Since this book is primarily practice oriented, we hope that much of the information in this book will help you in your everyday life in Spain and especially when buying your property. The information related to the purchase of real estate is valid throughout Spain, while sections relating to the rental of holiday rooms must be complemented by the current legal regulations of the corresponding Autonomous Community.

While our experience in buying property in Spain strongly recommends looking for professional advice in both due diligence and sales processing, the checklist at the end of this book can serve as a guide and as a safeguard. Tips tailored to the specific case are especially recommended where you answer "no" on the checklist. If you answer all sections with "yes" or if you are clear about the consequences for "no", you can basically carry out the sales process with ease,

 After signing the notarial deed of sale, it generally takes up to a week to receive the original notarial deed. Then you can use this time to prepare the payment of the corresponding taxes. If you have doubts about the calculation, your lawyer or tax advisor can advise you regarding the tax relief that differs from each Autonomous Community and generally prepare the corresponding tax return. If there are problems with the Land Registry after the presentation of the notarial deed of purchase, it is quite common for the Registrar to request improvements or believe that information is missing.

A corresponding administrative objection can be filed against these complaints, so in most cases it is easier and quicker for the notary to directly correct small complaints. In case of major complaints, both the notary and your lawyer can advise you on how to proceed.

Finally, it should be mentioned that the exchange of information between notaries, registries and the Autonomous Community can now be done electronically, but it is not necessary. Generally, there can be between 3 and 6 months between the signing of the notarial deed and the entry in the Land Registry.

Regarding this book, we personally await your criticism and suggestions and will be happy to answer your questions in person, by phone or by email. You can find more articles on relevant and current topics on our blog:

www.sspartners.es

If you have specific questions about legal and tax advice in Spain, we would be happy to help you personally from our law firm in Malaga, by phone or by email. We will also answer your phone call in English at the following phone numbers:

(+34) 951 12 00 69

(+49) 5105 60 89 964

m.santos@sspartners.es

Available at your library and on Amazon:

ISBN:
ISBN- 9798649308687

CHECKLIST REAL ESTATE PURCHASE

	Yes	No
Simple note		
The description of the Land Register property coincides with the seen property.		
The owners that appear in the Land Registry are the seller.		
There is not charges, as mortgages.		
If there are these have been economically canceled or are canceled at the signing act.		
Cadatral extract		
The description corresponds with the Cadatre.		
All the properties that are appreciated in the reality can be seen in the cadastral extract.		
The cadastral value is known, so the IBI can be calculated.		
Owner's community		
There is a community certificated stating that there are nor debts with the community.		
The Community Statutes are known.		

	Yes	No

Proof of payment IBI
There is proof of payment of IBI receipts for the last 2 years.

City Council Certificate of no urban infraction
There are no administrative procedures against the property

Reservation contract/arras contract

	Yes	No
The seller sign the contract and copies of the identity documents are attached.		
Double the deposit will be returned if the seller does not sign it.		
The contract establishes a right of withdrawal for loss of deposit (down payment).		
There is a certificate of bank ownership for the initial payment.		
The notary and the date for the notarial signature are determied directly.		

Before the notarial signature

	Yes	No
The NIE is available and is valid for the date scheduled for the notarial signature.		
If there are marital capitulations, these must be provided translated and with apostille.		

	Yes	*No*

The notaral sale contract

If the buyer or the seller do not speak Spanish, a translator has been appointed.		
The seller has is residence in Spain or the buyer retains the taxes.		
The marriage regime of the buyers is expressed (legal or with capitulations).		
The notary sends an electronic copy to the Land Registry (avoiding the registry lock).		

Payment taxes

Property transfer tax are pay within 30 days from the purchase.		

Registration in the Cadastre

The sealed notarial deed was registered in the Land Registry.		
An updated extract was issued in the Land Registry.		

Land Registry update

The property transfer was registered in the Land Registry.		

Printed in Great Britain
by Amazon